ONE NATION, MANY TRIBES

How Kids Live in Milwaukee's Indian Community

ONE NATION, MANY TRIBES

How Kids Live in Milwaukee's Indian Community

BY Kathleen Krull
PHOTOGRAPHS BY David Hautzig

Lodestar Books

DUTTON   NEW YORK

Frontispiece: **Kids at the Milwaukee Indian School powwow**

Library of Congress Cataloging-in-Publication Data
Krull, Kathleen.
One nation, many tribes: how kids live in
Milwaukee's Indian community/by Kathleen Krull;
photographs by David Hautzig.—1st ed.
p.   cm.—(A World of my own)
Includes index.
ISBN 0-525-67440-3
1. Indian children—Wisconsin—Milwaukee—Social life and customs—Juvenile literature.   2. Indians of North America—Wisconsin—Milwaukee—Social life and customs—Juvenile literature.   3. Indians of North America—History—Juvenile literature.   I. Hautzig, David, ill.   II. Title   III. Series: Krull, Kathleen.
World of my own.
E78.W8K78   1995
977.5'9500497—dc20   93-39538   CIP   AC

"4 977.595" per SM 10/97

Published in the United States by Lodestar Books,
an affiliate of Dutton Children's Books,
a division of Penguin Books USA Inc.,
375 Hudson Street, New York, New York 10014

Published simultaneously in Canada
by McClelland & Stewart, Toronto

Editor: Virginia Buckley   Designer: Joseph Rutt
Map by Matthew Bergman

Printed in Hong Kong   First Edition   10 9 8 7 6 5 4 3 2 1

to Patricia Laughlin and Robert Burnham of Milwaukee,
for wise counsel and salmon pasta

—K. K.

I dedicated an earlier book to some of my friends. Unfortunately,
I ran out of space. So in continuation . . . to Ellen Fuchida, Charles
Primus, the AV gang at DMB & B, George Thompson, Anthony and
Lauren Deen, Lou Manski, and Michele Pierson.

—D. H.

Acknowledgments

The author gratefully acknowledges the participation of Thirza Defoe and Shawnee Ford and their families, as well as the help of Mitch Walking Elk, Fred Bartelt, Michael Roberts, and especially Georgianna Ignace of the Milwaukee Indian Community School in Milwaukee, Wisconsin. Also helpful were Jane Botham, Children's Librarian, Milwaukee Public Library; Dr. Nancy Lurie, former curator of the Anthropology Department, Milwaukee Public Museum; Agnes Ljungblad; and Virginia Buckley of Lodestar. Thank you to Paul Brewer. Special thanks to Jennifer Lyons, Michele Rubin, and especially Susan Cohen, of Writers House.

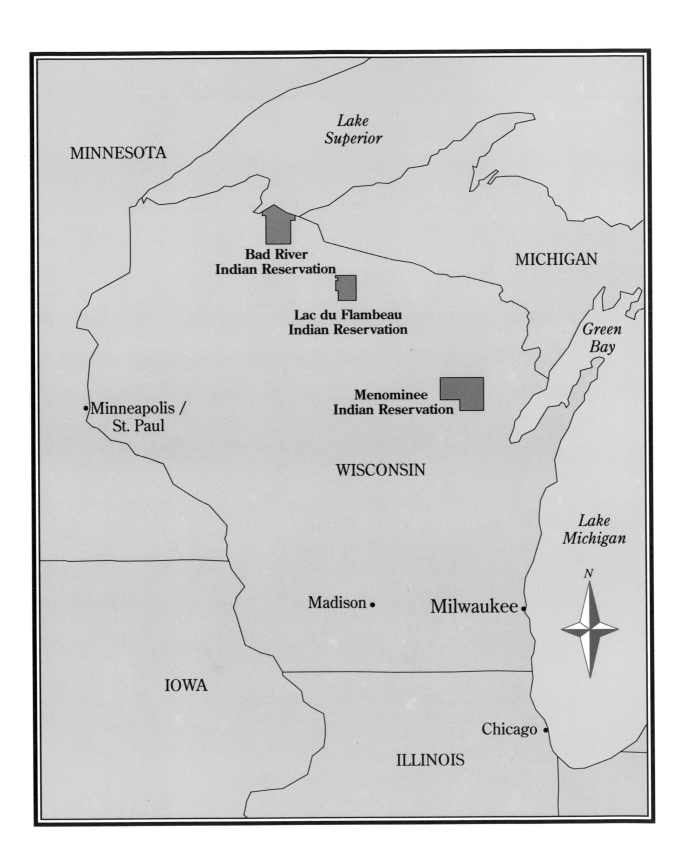

Thirza Defoe performing a traditional Indian hoop dance

T hirza Defoe, age eleven, can dance with sixteen hoops encircling her slim figure. She is a solo hoop dancer, skilled in a centuries-old Indian tradition. In her ceremonial black-and-white outfit, she performs on Indian reservations all around her home state of Wisconsin. She's danced in other states and as far away as Japan and the Olympics in Spain.

"Sometimes when I dance," she says, "non-Indians come around and make fun of me with those *whoo-whoo* war cries they see in movies. It makes me mad because they should know better. Kids should watch how we really dance, how we really act." Unless she is in a foreign country where she doesn't speak the language, as in Japan or Spain, she often goes over and tells those who tease that their imitations of Indians are mistaken. "Sometimes we sing along when we're dancing because we're enjoying ourselves—we might really like that song. We're not 'on the warpath' like in some old John Wayne cowboy movie."

Shawnee Ford, age twelve, started dancing as soon as he was able to walk. "A family friend played music and had me dance around a chair," he says. Now he performs at powwows, gatherings where Indians celebrate their culture. He wears his grass-dancing clothes, blue like the sky, or a red ceremonial outfit, parts of which he has made himself. He practices hard so as to become good enough to dance in competitions.

When he performs somewhere or goes on field trips, he frequently hears the same teasing whoops that Thirza gets. "Kids are reading too many books and watching too many cartoons," he says. He's inclined to ignore the teasing—"if you respond you just get in trouble"—though he sometimes has been provoked into arguments. He would like other kids to stop stereotyping, "even though there are still books and things around that say Indian people are savages. If you really got to know an Indian, you'd realize that person was just a normal human being."

Above: **Shawnee Ford is also an accomplished dancer.**

Facing page: **Shawnee's red ceremonial dancing outfit**

A welcome in five Indian languages

Shawnee and Thirza are regular kids who go to an unusual school—the Milwaukee Indian Community School in southern Wisconsin. Unlike Indian schools elsewhere, it is not in the country but rather in the heart of Milwaukee, the seventeenth largest city in the United States. Because it is not on a reservation like most other Indian schools, it is not limited to one tribe. It is open to the various tribes, or nations, living in Milwaukee. A sign at the front of the school greets you in five different languages: Ojibwa (pronounced *o-JIB-way*), Oneida (*o-NI-duh*), Menominee (*muh-NOM-uh-nee*), Winnebago (*win-uh-BAY-go*), and Potawatomi (*pot-uh-WOT-uh-mee*). Kids from these five tribes go to this, the only all-Indian school in the city.

Indians in Wisconsin

Once Indians were the only people in Wisconsin. Today, they account for a fraction of the state's population—some forty thousand out of five million people. The majority of Wisconsin's Indians are Ojibwa. This tribe inhabits six of the ten reservations within the state, all of them in northern Wisconsin. The tribe is also known as Chippewa, which is considered a less accurate name.

As in other states, more than half of Wisconsin's Indian population lives in the cities, particularly in Milwaukee, the biggest city. It is hard to find one Milwaukee neighborhood that is particularly Indian; the active Indian community is scattered, with many agencies to assist them.

Indian street and place names all around are reminders to everyone that the Milwaukee area is rich in Indian lore. The city began as an Indian trading post in 1674. The name Milwaukee *is from an Algonquian Indian word meaning "good land" or "great council place." Each of the several tribes still living in Wisconsin has a unique history.*

Indian elders are sources of each tribe's unique history.

Another unusual thing about this school is its financing. Milwaukee is the only city in the United States with a high-stakes bingo hall in the middle of it. The bingo hall is run by Potawatomi Indians, and in a special arrangement all the school's money comes out of the bingo proceeds. About one out of ten Indian children in Milwaukee attends the Indian Community School, and there is a long waiting list to get in. The school has major plans for expansion.

Proof of Indian heritage is a requirement for admission. All students must have a tribal identification number, which they get from the tribe they belong to. Like the majority of kids at the school, Thirza and Shawnee are both registered with the Ojibwa tribe. Shawnee, half Ojibwa and the rest Mexican and Comanche, was born in Milwaukee and has lived here all his life. Thirza is half Ojibwa and half Oneida. Although she was born in Milwaukee, she lived for three years on an Ojibwa reservation.

Money from the Potawatomi bingo hall supports the school.

Ojibwa History

The Ojibwa were one of the largest and most powerful tribes in all of North America. They were known for their sense of humor, reserve, and skill in battle. The name Ojibwa *may come from a certain style of puckered seam in the tribe's moccasins or from a word meaning "those who make pictographs"* (pictures that record information).

The Ojibwa were hunters of deer, ducks, and fish; farmers who grew corn, beans, and pumpkins; and gatherers of wild rice, nuts, berries, and herbs for medicine. They collected maple syrup, which they used to sweeten practically everything. They built wigwams and canoes from birchbark. Rituals like the naming ceremony, the vision quest, the society of medicine (midewewin), the marriage ceremony, and the ritual of the dead unified the scattered villages.

The Ojibwa tribe's first encounter with whites was with the French furriers in the early 1600s. One hundred years later, the Ojibwa were no longer self-sufficient. Fur trading with the Europeans led them to hunt more than was necessary; as a result, they lost many traditional survival skills.

In early wars, the Ojibwa fought on the side of the British against the American rebels. When the British withdrew in 1815, the Americans forced the Ojibwa to forfeit much of their land.

In 1968, three Ojibwa founded the American Indian Movement (AIM), an organization active in fighting for Indian rights. The most famous Ojibwa, however, the American poet Henry Wadsworth Longfellow's Hiawatha, was not a real person.

Today there are approximately two hundred thousand Ojibwa, living primarily in the midwestern states and in Canada.

Above: **Tepees at the Milwaukee Indian School**

Facing page: **In addition to science and English, Shawnee studies drumming**.

Their school goes out of its way to instill Indian culture into every aspect of its curriculum. Children learn to have pride in being Indian—the word increasingly preferred over *Native American,* which some now consider a dated term invented by whites. Besides the usual academic subjects, children learn the history of Indians in the United States, drumming (kids make their own drums with deerskin), dancing, singing, arts and crafts, and traditional ceremonies. In studying Indian languages, students are helping to preserve them; outside of schools like this, some four out of five Indian languages are dying.

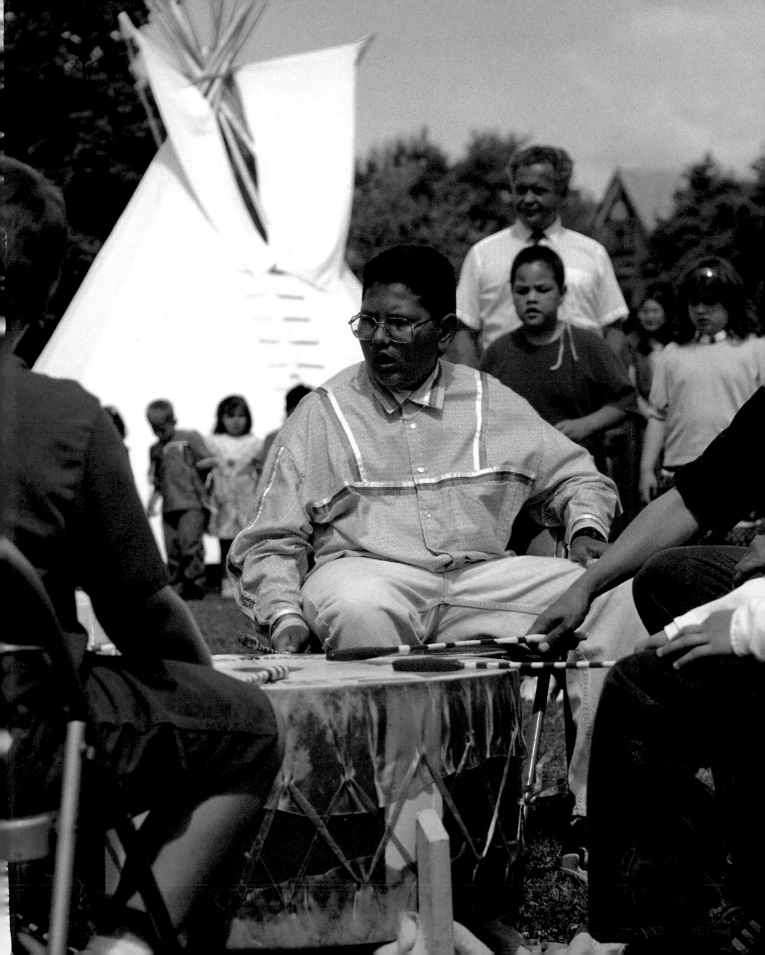

All of these subjects are taught from an intertribal perspective that emphasizes the universal features of the Indian world. Indians are different from any other ethnic group in the United States in that they are not considered immigrants. After being in the Wisconsin region, say, for as long as ten thousand years, they feel a closeness to the animals and plants from the area. These ties often have a deep, spiritual meaning, which is evident in the traditional Indian reverence for all things in nature.

Indians have lived amid this region's scenery for thousands of years.

Kids learn moccasin-making and other Indian crafts.

Kids at the school learn to think of themselves as Indian first and part of a tribe or nation second—they are nations within a nation. Kids from tribes that may have had fierce conflicts in the past now work side by side at the same computers and learn how to make the same kinds of moccasins.

If tribal rivalry does still exist, it is usually more evident among adults. Shawnee knows some people who hold grudges about what's gone on between two tribes. "But my mom teaches me that you can't live in the past," he says. "You have to live where you are." Kids treat rivalry more as a source of humor and use it to make fun of each other, according to Shawnee. "An Ojibwa kid could tell an Oneida kid, 'Hey, I saw one of those famous Oneida eagles—while pointing to an ordinary pigeon. Then the kid might laugh and walk away. It's not serious."

Shawnee enjoys playing games with his friends.

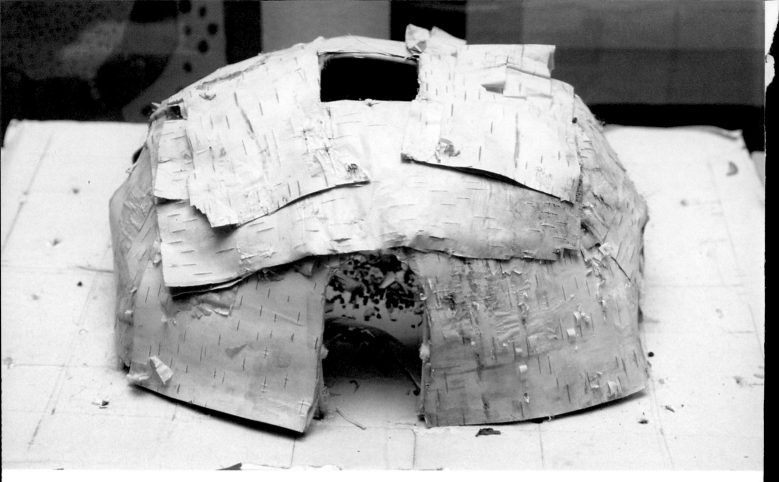

Shawnee built a model of a wigwam for a science project . . .

Before he came to this school, Shawnee didn't know very much about his heritage. Now he hopes he never has to transfer. "At a public school, they don't teach you your culture, your language. Here they teach us our background, so we know who we are, who our ancestors were, what they did, how they survived." Shawnee learns Indian ways even in academic classes. For his science fair project this year, he built models of a wigwam and tepee—two traditional Indian structures—to test which held heat better. He then gave a complete explanation of how the tepee was the one able to do so.

It's the same in his social studies class, where he gets events from an Indian perspective. In public schools, his experience was that the only time most kids read about Indians was at Thanksgiving.

"Then the rest of the time we're invisible or not considered really human," he says.

"This school teaches us that we were here long before Columbus; he didn't discover us," says Shawnee. "When I first heard about Columbus's 'discovery,' it made me mad. But there's nothing I can do about it." He feels the same way about the history of wars and broken treaties between whites and Indians. "They tricked us," he says. "We didn't know the value of money, they knew we didn't, and they used that against us, and that's how they got our land." But this doesn't affect his own relationships with whites. "They're different people than the ones who did it," he says. "Today is today. Just live in peace now, that's basically all you can do."

and he was able to demonstrate that a tepee holds heat better than a wigwam.

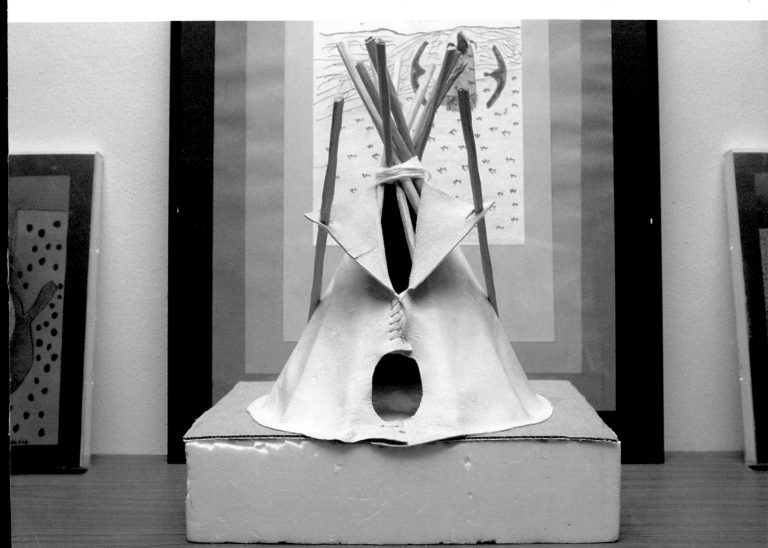

Contemporary Indians

Various government policies toward Indians have led to their gradual impoverishment. Families living on reservations, or tracts of land set aside for them, are more than twice as likely to live below the poverty level than those who moved to the cities. In 1985, the life expectancy for men on reservations was only forty-five to forty-seven, and for women forty-eight to fifty-one. The teen suicide rate is three times the national average. Reservation conditions are often so miserable that they threaten the existence of whole tribes.

Tourism has been one of the few ways for reservations to bring in money. Since a 1988 law permitted tribes to operate casinos, some reservations have used gambling as a way to improve conditions. The casinos draw outsiders like magnets; in fact, slot machines on reservations in Wisconsin, Minnesota, and South Dakota are depleting the area's supply of quarters. Gambling in these areas, however, does not compare with that in Las Vegas, Atlantic City, and state lotteries, where the majority of gambling in the United States takes place.

More than 12 million Indians, speaking at least two hundred different languages, lived in North America when Columbus arrived in 1492. By 1900, after massacres, exposure to European diseases, and having almost all of their land taken away, there were only 250,000 Indians left. Though many languages and tribes have vanished forever, the Indian population is currently expanding, not shrinking, up to almost 2 million in 1990.

Above: **New housing on a reservation**

Left: **Older, substandard housing on an Indian reservation**

Shawnee's favorite cultural activity is the sweat lodge, a purification ceremony that takes place every month on the full moon. This is a spiritual cleansing, a time for various kinds of prayer, and, as Shawnee explains, "What you say in there can never be repeated outside." Interested outsiders are welcome at some Indian religious functions but not all. To reveal details is considered disrespectful to revered medicine men and women, to ancestors, and to the spirit world. Tribes are also wary of any commercialization of ritual prayers.

Everything about the sweat lodge has spiritual meaning. The two lodges—one for girls, one for boys—are built with four wooden shafts. Each shaft represents a stage of life: child, young adult, older adult, and death. Inside the lodges it's dark and hot. Steam comes from water poured over hot rocks. Boys wear shorts, and girls wear long T-shirts, but even so, the heat can be intense. "Sometimes it gets hard to breathe," says Shawnee. "Kids with asthma have to leave. Some kids get claustrophobic. You try not to think about the heat, and then your discomfort passes. But sometimes you just have to get out."

A sweat lodge at the school

Mitch Walking Elk directs the school's cultural activities.

Every new moon brings another popular activity, the pipe ceremony. Boys and girls sit in a circle, and Mitch Walking Elk, the
school's cultural director, passes a pipe around. In the pipe is tobacco
mixed with sage or red willow bark shavings. From its smoke, says
Shawnee, "all our prayers go up to Manitou," meaning the Great Spirit
or Mystery from which all things draw life. Inhaling the smoke is not
mandatory—"It can make some kids cough." Tobacco is a sacred
plant in Indian tradition. "This doesn't mean we're encouraged to
smoke cigarettes or anything," Shawnee says. And as important as Indian spiritual life is to him, he doesn't discount other religions. He was
baptized Christian and also goes to church. "I pray to God as well as to
the Great Spirit," he says.

Kids give demonstrations of traditional dancing at other schools.

Unlike the academic subjects, the cultural activities at the school are not graded, since they're thought to be an ongoing process. "You can never learn enough. You could be ninety years old and still learning," explains Shawnee. He, Thirza, and other students publicize Indian culture by giving presentations at schools in Milwaukee, demonstrating drumming, various kinds of dancing, and traditional outfits.

Besides the sweat lodge, Shawnee also likes what every kid likes, being outdoors on the playground. "When it's not too cold and muddy to go outside, we play basketball, volleyball, and kickball," he says. His favorite sport is football.

Thirza has learned much at this school that she didn't know before, especially about spiritual traditions, such as the sweat lodge and the pipe ceremony, and hands-on activities like making skirts.

Hoop-dancing, though, is something she learned on the reservation from a cousin. She has since had other teachers and also learns from exchanging moves with people she meets at powwows. She plans to keep dancing for a long

Shawnee playing his favorite game

time, learning new movements, even if it sometimes seems difficult. "With all the people staring," she says, "you get so nervous it's hard to think about your feet." She keeps her concentration by pretending she is alone and letting different pictures pop into her head. She thinks of the moves she's dancing and imagines things like a firefly, eagle, dragon, or four-leaf clover. She wears a very serious expression, and she's never fallen down during a performance.

Everything in the dance signifies something, especially the hoops. "The hoop is a circle of life," she explains, "from the time you're a baby until you die. You're dancing for people, helping them go through the circle, especially people who have been abused. You're healing the sacred hoop." Her father, an artist who works as a timekeeper at an Indian casino, makes her hoops. He used to make them of willow branches, which bend easily, but now he uses tubing from the hardware store. He places leaves from the sacred tobacco plant inside the tubes. This is a way of asking the Great Spirit to watch over Thirza so she doesn't trip.

Thirza is always learning new movements to add to her dances.

Thirza's father lives on a reservation several hours away. Her extended family includes her mother, a ceramics teacher who also works at the bingo hall; an aunt; her baby nephew, Jacob; and another nephew, Forrest, who is actually three years older and whom she thinks of as a brother. They live in a two-story house on a busy street on the south side of town. The area is primarily Polish and Latino. Her older brother, Milo, has his own place.

Thirza with her mother and baby nephew

Shawnee lives with his mother, who is chairperson of the board of directors at his school; his father; his pet ferret, Chagag (the Indian word for skunk); and five finches. They have a ranch-style house on a quiet street on the north side, in a mixed neighborhood of Latinos, blacks, whites, and Indians. Although Shawnee's three older sisters have their own homes, he has lots of contact with his nine nieces and nephews.

Shawnee and his father play with the ferret, Chagag.

Shawnee's father (left) **directs security at the school.**

Almost all the children take the bus to school, and they are picked up and dropped off where parents can see them. Because the surrounding area has not been the safest in the past, the school is highly security conscious. Shawnee's father, who is in charge of safety and security at the school, took extra precautions when it was found that several victims of serial killer Jeffrey Dahmer came from this neighborhood.

The school itself reports few discipline problems. When kids have troubles, teachers use the Indian way of dealing with them: Kids sit down in a talking circle with others whom they respect.

If a sign of vandalism appears, such as gang-related graffiti in a bathroom, the school counters it with after-school activities and by teaching kids about clans. Each Indian tribe is divided into clans. The Oneida have three, for example, clan members have different duties: they can be leaders, workers, or spiritual healers. Kids learn to research their family tree and to take pride in their particular clan, rather than in a gang. Shawnee, is a member of the Ojibwa bear clan; his grandmother gave him a bear claw in a mandala to remind him of his family history.

When Thirza feels sad or angry, she rides her bike to a certain tree near her house and climbs up to sit on its branches. According to Indian tradition, the spirits of ancestors inhabit things in nature, and for Thirza trees hold particular meaning. Not only does she love to climb them, she also believes that they contain spirits. "Your grandma or grandpa could be inside that tree."

Above: **Shawnee's bear claw mandala is full of family history**.

Left: **Thirza in her favorite tree**

One day, when friends were giving her a hard time for not choosing sides in an argument, she felt hurt and went to sit in her special tree place. After she sat and thought for a while, she felt better and went home. "It was like my grandpa was telling me that everything was going to be OK," she says. Thirza also enjoys collecting rocks and she has amassed a large number of them. Rocks have a spiritual meaning for her as well. She thinks of spirits inside her rocks and treats them with great care.

Thirza's rock collection holds special meaning for her.

Thirza visits reservations whenever she can.

With their own families, Shawnee and Thirza leave the city and visit reservations whenever their parents can get time off from work to make the several hours' drive. They visit with elderly relatives, paying respect and learning more about family history, something that all the relatives keep track of. Both Shawnee and Thirza are in demand as traditional dancers, and they are often invited to reservations to perform. Shawnee likes seeing old friends, like vendors who sell Indian jewelry, or other dancers. "I always run into six or seven guys I know."

But the biggest reason for a visit to a reservation is to attend a powwow. "That's like the biggest holiday of the year, definitely bigger than Christmas, New Year's, anything," says Shawnee. It is a social time, when Indian traditions are kept alive through singing, dancing, and drumming.

Indian Contributions to the World

After 1492, American Indians influenced the way the Old World ate, thought, bought and sold goods, built things, and practiced ecology. In their expertise with plants, they were the greatest farmers and pharmacists of their time.

In medicine, Indians had developed the world's most sophisticated knowledge of herbs. Back in Europe, doctors were still applying live leeches to suck blood out of patients. Indians' knowledge of medicine has formed the basis of the modern pharmacy.

In government, the Indians were a major influence on the thoughts of Benjamin Franklin (whose first diplomatic job was as Pennsylvania's Indian commissioner), George Washington, and others involved in shaping this country. Features of the Iroquois' governing methods found their way into the Constitution of the United States.

Probably nowhere is the Indian influence more obvious than in the foods we eat. Three-fifths of the foods now grown in the world were introduced by American Indians. Items like the potato, chocolate, chili pepper, chewing gum, and tobacco have not only changed diets, they have sometimes led to the rise (or fall) of whole countries. The potato, for example, became the staple food of Ireland, which went on to triple its population. When a blight caused crops to fail, millions of Irish left Ireland for the New World.

Shawnee appreciates that government reservations try to preserve the land. You could have bears in your backyard and lots of forest. But this doesn't make Shawnee wish that he lived on a reservation. "It would be too hard to adapt," he says. "I'm used to the big city, where there's lots of noise. The reservation is too quiet and sleepy." Besides his school, the thing he would miss most about life in the city is shopping at malls. He loves to shop at Northridge Mall, near his house, and eat at his favorite Italian restaurant there.

Shawnee likes pasta, particularly mostaccioli. With his family he often eats Indian dishes such as fry bread (dough fried in hot oil). He likes wild rice and knows all about its cultivation and harvesting; he will be going ricing for the first time soon. Family gatherings frequently feature venison meat. Because the deer was killed by his "heavy hunter" uncles on the reservation, it has special spiritual meaning.

Thirza also likes Italian food, especially pizza, but she enjoys Indian food the most. At powwows she eats Indian tacos, buffalo burgers, buffalo soup, and venison. Her one regret about her school is that it doesn't yet serve Indian food, just cold lunches.

Shawnee gets an allowance for doing chores around the house, and in the summer he mows lawns at the golf course next door. He either spends his money on little stuff like batteries and candy or saves up for video games to play with Nathaniel, an Ojibwa who has been his best friend since kindergarten. Shawnee collects video games and Indian music tapes he buys at powwows. He loves to read, especially historical novels and other fiction with lots of facts. Favorite authors include Scott O'Dell and Gary Paulsen, and he really liked Lynne Reid Banks's *The Indian in the Cupboard*—except for one bit of stereotyping. "The part where it's assumed that the Indian wants 'firewater' to drink, meaning liquor," he says, "that's the kind of thing you see in bad old movies."

Shawnee plays video games at the mall.

Squirt-gun fights between Thirza and Milo

Besides her allowance, Thirza earns money baby-sitting her nephew Jacob. She buys presents for people's birthdays, toys for herself, candy at the corner store, and fireworks. After school, she does homework, eats, plays Super Nintendo, watches TV, plays in the backyard, or goes to the park a block away. There she has squirt-gun battles with Milo and Forrest or plays with walkie-talkies. She likes shooting baskets and getting together with her best friend, Shenny, an Apache and Mohawk.

When she's not dancing, Thirza earns basketball trophies.

Thirza is probably the only eleven-year-old on her block reading Tennessee Williams's plays, which were written for adults. She studies the kids' roles for theater classes she takes at the Milwaukee Performing Arts Center, where she learns monologues, how to audition, mime, and do make-up. Her additional reading includes the Baby-sitters Club books, magic books, and spooky stories like Edgar Allan Poe's "The Black Cat." Her favorite songs are show tunes from musicals, though she likes powwow music as well.

Thirza and Shawnee are both concerned about the use of Indian or mock-Indian names for things like sports teams and commercial products: the Atlanta Braves, the Washington Redskins, Winnebago trailers, Chief Wahoo soda.

"I don't like it," says Thirza. "Imagine if the tables were turned, and we used whites' names for things. To pick a name like Crazy Horse Beer shows that whites think all Indians drink beer, when they don't really know who we are and what we do."

A video of herself that Thirza uses for auditions

**Dreams are significant in Indian tradition;
this dream-catcher hangs over Thirza's bed.**

Shawnee finds such stereotyping offensive, too, but he tries not to take it personally. "It's not aimed directly at me," he says. "I get more upset about other things, like living conditions on the reservations, which are kind of rough. People are poor. Casinos and bingo are helping, but people still need more help. Getting too excited about brand names takes attention away from the really important things."

Thirza and Shawnee both have other names, traditional Indian ones that were picked out especially for them to signify their identity within the Indian community. Thirza's Indian name, Sky Woman, was given by her grandmother, after she had a dream "about a lady coming from the sky." Shawnee's Indian name means Loud-Noise-in-the-Sky, and refers to thunder. It came from a vision that the medicine man on the reservation had, and does not mean that Shawnee was a particularly noisy baby. Sometimes, though, the names do fit. "I know a kid named Something-That-Makes-Noise," says Shawnee, "and he's, well, loud."

As symbolized by their two names, Thirza and Shawnee have two identities, one as typical American kids and another as representatives

Indian values play an important part in Shawnee's friendships.

of traditional Indian culture. Their plans for the future blend both worlds.

When he is older, Shawnee may work on a reservation. Because he enjoyed doing his science fair project so much, he thinks he might like to be an architect. His dream is to go to reservations and build different things for them—"playgrounds, better housing, community buildings, grocery stores, places the Indians don't have and have to go into town for." He believes that his success in life will depend on keeping Indian values. In his friendships with others, he tries to apply a saying he hears from his mother and grandmother: "Don't walk ahead of me because I may not follow. Don't walk behind me because I may not lead you right. Just walk on the side of me and be my friend."

Shawnee doesn't know if he will get married, but if he does, he would prefer to marry another Indian, so that they could raise their kids in the traditional culture. Ultimately, however, Shawnee says, "If you love someone, their color or race doesn't matter."

Thirza is already passing her special knowledge on directly. Just as she learned hoop-dancing from one cousin, so she is now teaching what she knows to another cousin, age seven. Her career choice is firm—she is going to be an actor. She has been in plays and musicals such as *Annie, The Best Christmas Pageant Ever,* and *The Wizard of Oz* since she was little. She has already starred in her first movie, an educational video called *People of the Forest.* She probably will not live on a reservation for the simple reason that "no acting jobs are there." Wisconsin is also too cold for her taste; she would prefer somewhere warm, like California or Florida.

As for marriage and children, Thirza expects to be too busy with acting. "I like kids but I don't want any of my own," she says. "I would want them to live normal lives, to see their mama instead of having someone else take care of them."

Thirza playing kickball—she expects to be just as active in the future.

Although many children learn about Indian culture from their relatives, the Milwaukee Indian Community School is more often the source of knowledge. "It's possible," says Mitch Walking Elk, "for kids who don't get this training to assimilate into the non-Indian, white world—to become what is called successful, like lawyers, doctors. But many do not, because they haven't found out who they are. When you know who you are, you can become a well-rounded, good person, helpful to your community."

Just as more realistic publicity about Indians, like the movie *Dances with Wolves,* has inspired many non-Indians to value Native American culture, a number of younger Indians are becoming more interested in maintaining it. "Kids here have an important job to do," says Mitch Walking Elk, "and that is what our ancestors did—defending the land and a way of life."

Thirza and Shawnee, it seems clear, are doing their job even now.

Mitch Walking Elk leads drummers at a school powwow.

For Further Reading

Ancona, George. *Powwow.* San Diego: Harcourt Brace, 1993.

Clifton, James A. *The Potawatomi.* New York: Chelsea House, 1987.

Duvall, Jill. *The Oneida.* Chicago: Childrens Press, 1991.

Green, Rayna. *Women in American Indian Society.* New York: Chelsea House, 1992.

Hirschfelder, Arlene, and Beverly Singer. *Rising Voices: Writings of Young Native Americans.* New York: Scribner, 1992.

Hoyt-Goldsmith, Diane. *Cherokee Summer.* New York: Holiday House, 1993.

Keegan, Marcia. *Pueblo Boy: Growing Up in Two Worlds.* New York: Cobblehill, 1991.

Lurie, Nancy. *Wisconsin Indians.* Madison: State Historical Society of Wisconsin, 1980 (for adults).

Nabokov, Peter, editor. *Native American Testimony: A Chronicle of Indian-White Relations from Prophecy to the Present, 1492-1992.* New York: Viking, 1992 (for adults).

Osinski, Alice. *The Chippewa.* Chicago: Childrens Press, 1987.

Ourada, Patricia. *The Menominee.* New York: Chelsea House, 1990.

Tanner, Helen Hornbeck. *The Ojibwa.* New York: Chelsea House, 1992.

Waldman, Carl. *Encyclopedia of Native American Tribes.* New York: Facts on File, 1988.

Weatherford, Jack. *Indian Givers: How the Indians of the Americas Transformed the World.* New York: Crown, 1988 (for adults).

Wolfson, Evelyn. *From the Earth to Beyond the Sky: Native American Medicine.* Boston: Houghton Mifflin, 1993.